DON'T DROWN WITH THE CROWD

— FORTUNE OMOSOLA

FORTUNE OMOSOLA © 2023

ISBN (Paperback) - 978-1-917267-26-7

ISBN (E-Book) - 978-1-917267-27-4

Published by Nubian Republic on behalf of Palmwine Publishing Limited Nigeria

Email: info@palmwinepublishing.com

Address- UK: 86-90, Paul Street, London EC2A 4NE

Address-Nigeria: 1A Jos Road Bukuru, Plateau State, Nigeria.

www.palmwinepublishing.com
www.raffiapress.com
www.nuciferaanalysis.com

Table of Contents

CHAPTER 1

MENTALITY MONSTER

There is a reason why there is a winner in most games of football - Mentality. The winner wants the 3 points at all cost, the second best is satisfied with whatever outcome.

In anything, in the minutiae of it, people love to win, maybe not everyone, but if you love to, you need a mentality for it.

Mentality is everything. It's the key to success, the driving force behind achievement, and the foundation of resilience. With the right mindset, anything is possible. That's why becoming a "mentality monster" is so important.

If you want to be a mentality monster, you need to start by adopting a growth mindset. This means believing that your abilities can be developed and improved over time, rather than believing that they are fixed and unchangeable. Take inspiration from figures like Michael Jordan, who famously said, "I've failed over and over and over again in my life. And that is why I succeed." By embracing failure as a learning opportunity, you can cultivate a growth mindset and become unstoppable.

Another key aspect of being a mentality monster is having a strong sense of purpose. You need to know what you're working towards and why it matters to you. Look to figures like Oprah Winfrey, who has said, "The biggest adventure you can ever take is to live the life of your dreams." By setting ambitious goals and working towards them with purpose and passion, you can achieve incredible things.

Of course, being a mentality monster isn't just about having the right mindset - it's also about taking action. You need to be willing to put in the work and make sacrifices in pursuit of your goals. Take inspiration from figures like Dwayne "The Rock" Johnson, who has said, "Success isn't always about greatness. It's about consistency. Consistent hard work leads to success. Greatness will come." By consistently putting in the effort, you can achieve greatness.

At the same time, it's important to be flexible and adaptable. Life is unpredictable, and you need to be able to pivot and adjust your plans when necessary. Look to figures like Serena Williams, who has said, "I think in life you should work on yourself until the day you die." By staying open to new experiences and constantly seeking to improve yourself, you can overcome any obstacle.

Being a mentality monster also means being resilient in the face of setbacks and adversity. You need to be able to bounce back from failure and keep pushing forward. Take inspiration from figures like J.K. Rowling, who has said, "It is impossible to live without failing at something, unless you live so cautiously that you might as well not have lived at all - in which case, you fail by default." By embracing failure as a natural part of the journey and using it as a learning opportunity, you can become stronger and more resilient than ever before.

Ultimately, being a mentality monster is about being true to yourself and staying true to your values. Look to figures like Michelle Obama, who has said, "Just do what works for you, because there will always be someone who thinks differently." By staying true to yourself and staying true to your goals, you can achieve incredible things and become a true mentality monster. So go out there and make it happen - you have this.

You are built to win, enforce it.

CHAPTER 2

WHAT MAKES YOU?

What makes a good writer? books!

A good teacher? experience!

a good learner? attention.

There is a price for anything worth the buy.

Becoming a skilled writer, teacher, or learner is not a walk in the park. It takes hard work, dedication, and a willingness to learn and improve continuously.

As with anything in life, there is a price to pay for achieving success. However, there are certain principles and strategies that can give you a head start towards your goals.

For instance, to become a good writer, one must read widely and regularly. Reading exposes you to different writing styles, genres, and ideas. The direction is to help you learn how to express yourself in a clear, concise, and engaging manner. Just like a chef who tastes different dishes to learn how to cook better, a writer must read books to improve their writing skills.

Similarly, a good teacher is not just someone with years of experience. Teaching requires constant learning and self-improvement. A teacher who relies on their experience alone may become outdated and ineffective. A good teacher must stay up-to-date with the latest research, trends, and best practices in their field. Just like a doctor who continues to learn new medical techniques, a teacher must keep learning to be a successful educator.

In the same texture, a good learner must be soldier ready to pay attention. Learning requires focus, dedication, and active engagement with the material. You cannot expect to learn something if you are not paying attention. Just like an athlete who trains their body to perform at its best, a learner must train the mind to absorb information and retain it effectively.

Overall, attaining the acme in any area of life requires hard work, dedication, and a willingness to learn and improve continuously.

There are no shortcuts to achieving goals; the easy way often leads to disastrous endings. By following the right principles and strategies, you can give yourself a head start towards success and achieve your full potential.

But, there are no buts.

CHAPTER 3

SANGFROID

To be calm when others are howling is a gift.

There is a quiet appeal that greets a discreet mind who is careful to perceive, to say, to hold firm even when there is pressure.

To remain discreet is the hallmark of a few, to review their telling of it before public knowledge.

One of the lessons of life's success is not revealing much because the order of such steps are complex. Arnold White says, "Envy yourself in silence and come in agreement with your moments". In other words, there are things better left unsaid.

The ability to remain calm and collected in the face of chaos is a highly coveted trait. It's a quality that few possess, but one that is highly admired. When everyone else is panicking and howling, the person with sangfroid is able to remain composed and rational. This ability can be especially useful in high-pressure situations, such as a crisis or emergency.

In popular culture, there are numerous examples of characters who embody sangfroid. One such character is James Bond, the iconic British spy. Known for his cool, calm demeanor and his ability to think on his feet, Bond is the epitome of sangfroid. He's able to stay focused and level-headed, even in the most dangerous and stressful situations.

Another pop culture icon who exemplifies sangfroid is the character of Sherlock Holmes. With his razor-sharp mind and uncanny ability to solve even the most perplexing mysteries, Holmes is a model of composure and poise. He's able to remain calm and collected, even when faced with seemingly insurmountable obstacles.

In the world of sports, there are many examples of athletes who display sangfroid on the field or court. One such athlete is basketball superstar LeBron James. Known for his ability to rise to the occasion in clutch situations, James is able to remain calm and focused, even when the game is on the line.

In business, sangfroid is a highly valued trait. Successful entrepreneurs such as Steve Jobs and Elon Musk are known for their ability to remain calm and collected, even in the face of setbacks and obstacles. They are able to maintain their composure and stay focused on their goals, even when the road ahead seems rough.

Whether it's in the world of entertainment, sports, business, or everyday life, the ability to remain calm and collected in the face of chaos is a skill that can be invaluable. By cultivating this quality, we can all strive to be more like the heroes and role models who embody sangfroid in their daily lives.

Stay Calm.

CHAPTER 4

YOUR WEAKNESS

Weakness could be anything. It is a distraction meant to limit you in a crowded world with limited opportunities.

People indulge in their weaknesses without knowing it until it saturates their space and dissipates all the positive energy they have to thrust forward.

Be aware that weakness is a universal human experience. We all have our Achilles' heels, whether it's a tendency to procrastinate, a fear of public speaking, or an addiction to junk food. These weaknesses can be a major distraction in a world that's full of opportunities and challenges.

They can hold us back from achieving our goals and reaching our full potential.

One of the tricky things about weakness is that it can be hard to recognize. We might not even realize we have a weakness until it's already taken hold of us. It's like a weed that starts as a tiny seed, but then grows and spreads until it's taken over the whole garden. Before we know it, our weakness has become a major obstacle in our lives.

But there is hope! The antidote to weakness is discipline. Just as a doctor prescribes medicine to cure an illness, discipline can help us overcome our weaknesses and become stronger, more resilient versions of ourselves. Discipline is like a muscle that we can exercise and strengthen over time.

Of course, building discipline is easier said than done. It requires a lot of hard work, patience, and self-awareness. We have to be willing to confront our weaknesses head-on and make a commitment to change. It's not a quick fix, but it is a long-term solution that can have a transformative effect on our lives.

The good news is that discipline can be contagious. When we start to build discipline in one area of our lives, it can spread to other areas as well. We might find that we have more energy, focus, and motivation to tackle other challenges and pursue new opportunities.

Think of discipline like a domino effect. When you line up a row of dominoes, all it takes is a gentle nudge to set them in motion. Each domino knocks over the next one, and so on, until the whole row has fallen.

This is no motivation, but be rest assured that the antidote to weakness is discipline.

CHAPTER 5

CROWD VALIDATION CAN BE HARMFUL, TRUST YOURSELF

Trust is one of the most important and valuable commodities in life. It is something that cannot be easily regained once lost, and therefore should be treated with the utmost care and respect. However, in today's world, it seems that people are more interested in seeking validation from the crowd, rather than trusting in themselves.

The rush for validation has become so prevalent that people are willing to lower their standards, compromise their values and beliefs, and even sacrifice their own happiness just to fit in with the crowd. It's like giving away a prized possession to a group of swine who have no appreciation for its value. But the truth is, the crowd is effervescent and fickle, always moving on to the next shiny thing. Don't get carried away with their whims and fancies.

Why not trust yourself, trust your instincts, your judgment, your intuition?

Don't let the opinions of others drown out your own inner voice. Your perspective and experiences are unique, and that's what makes them valuable. It's like having a rare painting that is one-of-a-kind. You wouldn't let the opinions of others dictate its value, would you? Similarly, you should not let the crowd's opinions dictate your worth or decision-making.

Stop making comparisons that limit your chances of staying in charge. It's easy to get caught up in comparing ourselves to others, especially in today's world of social media where we see curated highlights of everyone else's lives. But this only leads to feelings of inadequacy, self-doubt, and ultimately, a lack of trust in ourselves. Instead, focus on creating your own memories, experiences, and happiness. Be authentic to who you are and what you stand for, rather than trying to conform to the expectations of others.

Trusting yourself is like having a compass that always points in the right direction. You don't need to follow the crowd blindly or second-guess yourself constantly. You have the power to chart your own course, make your own decisions, and navigate through life on your own terms. It's like being the captain of your own ship, sailing towards your own destination, rather than being a passenger on someone else's journey.

In this contemporary times, the crowd efferves on evanescence and immediately turn to the next. So, don't get carried away. In other words, do you, create your own memories and be happy. Stop making comparisons that limits your chances at staying in charge.

Trust is a precious commodity that should be guarded and cherished. Don't give it away to the swine of the crowd. Trust in yourself, your instincts, your experiences, and your unique perspective. Don't let the opinions of others dictate your worth or decision-making. Instead, focus on creating your own memories, experiences, and happiness. Trust yourself like a compass that always points in the right direction, and be the captain of your own ship!

CHAPTER 6

SELECTIVE OUTRAGE

I once saw a headline performance by popular Comedian, Chris Rock; it was on Netflix and charge through what he described as "Selective Outrage". It was an adrenaline rush that sparked scenes of how people defined their truths or what's important from the threshold of personal sentiments and force it down the throat of the society.

What exactly is selective outrage?

It is the tendency of individuals or groups to express strong emotions such as anger, indignation or moral disgust, only when certain issues or incidents align with their personal or group interests, beliefs or values, while ignoring or minimizing similar issues or incidents that do not. This phenomenon can be seen in various domains, such as politics, social justice, media coverage, and everyday interactions. Selective outrage can have significant consequences for the individuals, groups, and societies involved, and it raises important ethical and psychological questions about our capacity for fairness, empathy, and moral reasoning.

One example of selective outrage is political polarization, in which people tend to defend their own political party or ideology even when it engages in unethical or harmful actions, while condemning the opposing party or ideology for similar actions.

This phenomenon has been observed in various contexts, such as the U.S. presidential elections, where people tend to overlook or rationalize the flaws and misdeeds of their preferred candidate, while magnifying or distorting the flaws and misdeeds of the opposing candidate.

As the philosopher Martha Nussbaum notes, "Political polarization is not just a matter of different opinions, but also of different emotions and narratives that generate a sense of identity and belonging that can override the facts and the common good."

Another example of selective outrage is social justice activism, in which people focus on certain forms of oppression or discrimination, such as racism, sexism, homophobia, or ableism, while neglecting or downplaying other forms of oppression or discrimination, such as classism, ageism, or discrimination against people with non-normative sexual or gender identities. As the writer Roxane Gay observes, "Intersectionality, the idea that multiple forms of oppression intersect and compound each other, is a vital aspect of social justice, but it also exposes the limitations and blind spots of selective outrage." Gay argues that social justice activism should aim to address all forms of oppression, even if they are not as visible or sensationalized as others.

Selective outrage can also occur in the media, where certain events or issues receive extensive coverage and public attention, while others are overlooked or marginalized. For example, in the aftermath of the terrorist attacks on September 11, 2001, the media focused heavily on the threat of Islamic terrorism and the wars in Afghanistan and Iraq, while paying little attention to other forms of violence, such as domestic terrorism, police brutality, or the humanitarian crisis in Gaza. This imbalance can perpetuate stereotypes and stigmatize certain groups, as the journalist Glenn Greenwald argues: "The selective outrage of the media reflects and reinforces the biases and prejudices of society, and it shapes public opinion and policy."

Selective outrage can also affect interpersonal relationships, where people may react strongly to perceived slights or offenses that are consistent with their personal identity or values, while dismissing or minimizing the feelings or experiences of others. For example, a person who is passionate about environmental issues may become enraged when someone litters in their presence, while disregarding or belittling the concerns of someone who is affected by systemic racism or poverty. This can create resentment and division, as the psychologist Steven Pinker notes: "Selective outrage can lead to a self-righteousness that divides people into competing tribes, rather than fostering mutual understanding and compassion."

The roots of selective outrage can be traced to various psychological and sociological factors, such as cognitive biases, group identity, moral reasoning, and social norms. One of the most common cognitive biases that contributes to selective outrage is confirmation bias, which refers to the tendency to seek, interpret, and remember information that confirms one's preexisting beliefs or values, while ignoring or discounting information that contradicts them. This bias can lead to distorted perceptions of reality and a lack of empathy or curiosity for alternative perspectives.

Are you selective in your outrage?

CHAPTER 7

FRIENDSHIP

Friendship is an expensive investment, whichever form it takes.

I have come to understand what true friendship means and why anything less of it should be discarded. Most of us boast of friends that can be better placed as acquaintances. These sorts are too distant, sprained and artificial, at every instance or more, they rock you psychologically. They are better off detached and displaced.

On the flipside are accidental friendship, the types that masks as real ones but can hardly survive the true test of staying in form. They cut you loose but are short-lived.

Friendship is one of the most important relationships that we can develop in our lives. A true friend is someone who is there for us through thick and thin, who supports us in our goals and dreams, and who challenges us to be the best version of ourselves. Conversely, a bad friendship can be toxic and destructive, draining our energy and leaving us feeling unsupported and unfulfilled. In this essay, I will explore the importance of true friendship for self-development and why bad friendships can lead to destruction.

First and foremost, true friendships are crucial for self-development because they provide us with a sense of belonging and connection. As human beings, we are social creatures, and we need to feel that we are part of a larger community. True friends give us a sense of belonging and help us to feel connected to something larger than ourselves. In the words of William Shakespeare, "A friend is one that knows you as you are, understands where you have been, accepts who you have become, and still, gently allows you to grow."

True friendships also provide us with support and encouragement when we need it most. Life can be tough at times, and we all need someone to lean on when things get challenging. True friends are there to support us through the ups and downs of life, providing us with a shoulder to cry on and a listening ear. They encourage us to pursue our goals and dreams, and help us to overcome obstacles and challenges along the way.

In addition to providing us with support and encouragement, true friendships also challenge us to be the best version of ourselves. True friends are not afraid to tell us when we are wrong, or to call us out when we are not living up to our potential. They push us to grow and develop as individuals, and help us to see our blind spots and areas for improvement.

Conversely, bad friendships can be incredibly destructive to our self-development. A bad friend is someone who is self-centered, manipulative, and draining. They may use us for their own purposes, or bring us down with their negativity and drama. In the words of Eleanor Roosevelt, "One's philosophy is not best expressed in words; it is expressed in the choices one makes. In the long run, we shape our lives and we shape ourselves. The process never ends until we die. And, the choices we make are ultimately our own responsibility."

Bad friendships can lead to destruction in a number of ways. They can drain us of our energy and leave us feeling unsupported and unfulfilled. They can also hold us back from pursuing our goals and dreams, or lead us down a path of self-destructive behavior. In extreme cases, bad friendships can even lead to abuse, betrayal, or other forms of harm.

As we navigate our relationships with others, it is important to be mindful of the impact that our friendships have on our lives, and to choose our friends wisely. As the saying goes, "Show me your friends and I'll show you your future."

True friendships start off gradually, help your rhythm, are engaging, truthful, emotionally considerate and are more often than not symbiotic on both sides. If you don't find yours refreshing, cancel. Don't hide under servitude and press your own neck. The fewer your friends, the better or none at all.

I have thrown away friends because I do all the caring; I put in too much effort when the other person apparently doesn't give a damn. Sometimes, a friend can change but when it starts affect communication and other genes that establishes that connection, break off! it will only keep you in a mental prison if you don't.

True friends, bond, mix, accommodate and make better. Such connections are not restricted by time, place, rather there is energy by time to finetune it. Is not one sided, too demanding or smarmy. There are some friends who see you as a competitor and seize every opportunity to strive with you, where is the balance as expected?

Humans have their variations and you must call it from afar before you stick your neck in. Adios!

CHAPTER 8

EXERCISES ARE REFRESHING!

Exercises help you find a balance, don't discard the thought of it or treat it trivially when you opt in. While some people take it seriously, others don't but try to find time to exhale with it in a world where psychosomatic issues are in abundance.

Exercise is like a tune-up for your body: Just like how your car needs regular maintenance to keep it running smoothly, your body needs exercise to stay healthy and functioning optimally. Exercise helps to strengthen your muscles, increase your flexibility, and improve your overall physical health.

"Physical fitness is not only one of the most important keys to a healthy body, it is the basis of dynamic and creative intellectual activity." - John F. Kennedy: This quote by former US President John F. Kennedy highlights the link between physical fitness and mental sharpness. Exercise not only keeps your body healthy but also boosts your mental clarity and productivity.

Exercise is like a reset button for your mind: When you're feeling stressed or overwhelmed, exercise can help to clear your mind and reset your focus. Exercise releases endorphins, which are feel-good chemicals that help to reduce stress and boost your mood.

"The first wealth is health." - Ralph Waldo Emerson: This quote by philosopher Ralph Waldo Emerson highlights the importance of prioritizing our health above all else. Without our health, we cannot fully enjoy the other aspects of our lives.

Exercise is like a natural energy booster: Instead of reaching for that cup of coffee or energy drink, try going for a brisk walk or doing a quick workout. Exercise helps to increase blood flow and oxygenation to your brain and muscles, providing a natural energy boost that lasts throughout the day.

Exercise is like a way to connect with others: Joining a fitness class or sports team is a great way to connect with others who share your interests and goals. Exercising with others can provide a sense of community and support, helping you to stay motivated and committed to your fitness routine.

"Those who think they have not time for bodily exercise will sooner or later have to find time for illness." - Edward Stanley: This quote by politician Edward Stanley highlights the consequences of neglecting our physical health. By making exercise a priority, we can prevent illness and disease, and save ourselves time and money in the long run.

Exercise is like an investment in your future: By staying active and healthy, we can increase our lifespan and improve our quality of life as we age. Exercise helps to reduce the risk of chronic diseases such as heart disease, diabetes, and osteoporosis, and can help us to maintain our independence and vitality as we grow older.

Exercise is like a way to challenge yourself: Setting fitness goals and working towards them can provide a sense of accomplishment and boost your self-esteem. Whether it's running a marathon or mastering a new yoga pose, exercise provides endless opportunities for personal growth and achievement.

Exercise is like a habit that can transform your life: By making exercise a daily habit, you can transform your physical and mental health, boost your energy and productivity, and enhance your overall quality of life. As writer James Clear notes, "Every action you take is a vote for the type of person you wish to become."

By choosing to prioritize exercise, you are choosing to become a healthier, stronger, and more resilient version of yourself.

CHAPTER 9

READ, NO ONE READS AGAIN

It's a GenZ world, everyone is carried away. The paper barely crinkles, the pages barely flips, everyone is steaming on social pages and barely scratching anything. That's the picture of a crazy world tearing sensitivities apart and killing of the desire to gain or fatten our knowledge with books.

In the age of instant gratification, where information is readily available at our fingertips, it's easy to forget the value of reading. Yet, reading is more important now than ever before. With technology and the internet rapidly changing the way we live, work, and communicate, reading provides an opportunity to escape the noise of the digital world and enter into a quiet space where we can expand our minds and broaden our perspectives.

While the convenience of technology has made reading easier, it has also led to a culture of impatience and distraction. The average attention span has decreased dramatically in recent years, making it harder for people to concentrate on a book for extended periods of time. But the benefits of reading are immense, including increased cognitive function, improved empathy, and reduced stress.

Reading can also be a form of self-care, providing a mental break from the stresses of everyday life. When we immerse ourselves in a good book, we can forget about our problems and experience a sense of relaxation and calm. It's like taking a mini vacation without ever leaving your home.

One of the greatest benefits of reading is its ability to expand our knowledge and understanding of the world around us. Books can take us to far-off lands, introduce us to new ideas, and challenge our beliefs. They can also serve as a tool for personal growth, helping us to develop new skills and strengthen our existing ones.

As the famous quote goes, "The more that you read, the more things you will know. The more that you learn, the more places you'll go" (Dr. Seuss). Reading can take us on a journey of self-discovery and open up new avenues for exploration and personal development.

Furthermore, reading can also improve our communication skills, as it exposes us to new vocabulary, grammar, and syntax. This can be especially helpful for those who are learning a new language or seeking to improve their writing abilities.

It's important to note that reading doesn't have to be a solitary activity. Joining a book club or discussing a book with friends can add an element of socialization to the experience. It's a great way to connect with others and share perspectives on a shared interest.

Additionally, reading can have a positive impact on mental health. Studies have shown that reading can reduce stress and anxiety, increase empathy, and improve overall well-being (Bal, 2019). In fact, reading has been shown to be more effective at reducing stress than other relaxation techniques, such as listening to music or drinking a cup of tea (Rayner et al., 2012).

In today's fast-paced world, it's easy to get caught up in the hustle and bustle of everyday life. Reading provides an opportunity to slow down and reflect on what's truly important. It allows us to disconnect from the constant stimulation of technology and enter into a space of calm and introspection.

If you're looking for motivation to start reading, consider the words of the great philosopher, Aristotle: "The roots of education are bitter, but the fruit is sweet." While reading may require effort and discipline, the rewards are immeasurable. From expanded knowledge to improved mental health, reading offers a multitude of benefits.

If you're struggling to find the time to read, try setting aside a specific time each day for this activity. Whether it's during your morning coffee break or before bed, carving out even a small amount of time each day can make a significant impact on your reading habits.

Another way to motivate yourself to read is to set specific goals for yourself. Whether it's reading a certain number of books per month or completing a particular book series, having a concrete goal can help keep you on track and motivated.

There is no losing adding some muscles of knowledge to yourself, drown the noise by reading.

CHAPTER 10

WALK ALONE BUT DON'T FIGHT ALONE

Everyman is immersed in his own walk, in his life journey; he is alone even though he is gregarious. But, getting to one's target destination requires a joint effort, teaming up, extending a hand, reaching oit to people, getting involved. The way to the top requires a helping hand but you must decide alone. It is simple, yet, complex.

Have you ever heard the phrase "no man is an island"? It's true - we all need support and help from others at some point in our lives. However, the ultimate decision-making power lies with ourselves. We must walk alone in our journey of life, but that doesn't mean we have to fight alone. We can collaborate and team up with others to achieve our goals.

Think about it - when you're climbing a mountain, you may need a helping hand to get to the top. But, you're the one who has to make the decision to keep going and push through the difficulties. As motivational speaker Les Brown said, "You must be willing to do the things today others won't do in order to have the things tomorrow others won't have."

Walking alone means taking responsibility for our own actions and decisions. It means we can't blame anyone else if things don't go as planned. However, we don't have to face our challenges alone. We can seek advice and support from others who have been through similar situations. As author and speaker Simon Sinek said, "Working hard for something we don't care about is called stress. Working hard for something we love is called passion."

Collaboration and teamwork are important factors in achieving success. As the African proverb goes, "If you want to go fast, go alone. If you want to go far, go together." By working with others, we can pool our resources, share ideas, and accomplish more than we could on our own. However, we still have to take ownership of our own decisions and actions.

We shouldn't be afraid to ask for help when we need it. As former U.S. President Barack Obama said, "Don't be afraid to ask questions. Don't be afraid to ask for help when you need it. I do that every day. Asking for help isn't a sign of weakness, it's a sign of strength. It shows you have the courage to admit when you don't know something, and to learn something new."

Sometimes, it can be difficult to admit we need help. We may feel like we're burdening others or showing weakness. However, as author and speaker Brené Brown said, "Vulnerability is not weakness. And that myth is profoundly dangerous." Asking for help and being vulnerable can actually be a sign of strength.

We also need to be willing to help others when they need it. As writer and poet Maya Angelou said, "I've learned that people will forget what you said, people will forget what you did, but people will never forget how you made them feel." By extending a helping hand, we can make a positive impact on someone else's life and create a lasting impression.

Walking alone doesn't mean we have to isolate ourselves from others. It means we take ownership of our own journey while also seeking support and collaboration when necessary. As author and speaker Tony Robbins said, "People who succeed have momentum. The more they succeed, the more they want to succeed, and the more they find a way to succeed."

We all have the power to make a difference in our own lives and in the lives of others. As civil rights activist Rosa Parks said, "I have learned over the years that when one's mind is made up, this diminishes fear; knowing what must be done does away with fear." When we take ownership of our own decisions and actions, we can overcome our fears and achieve great things.

So, remember - walk alone but don't fight alone. Seek support and collaboration when necessary, but ultimately take ownership of your own journey. As author and speaker Jim Rohn said, "Take care of your body. It's the only place you have to live." Take care of yourself and your journey, and don't be afraid to live.

CHAPTER 11

GET ANGRY

It is the rage you conceive in certain moments that releases the needed adrenaline to make some life changing decisions. Enjoy the moments but don't be satisfied with yourself, there is a lot of value in pushing the limits.

Getting angry may seem like an unusual piece of advice, but as Bruce Lee once said, "Do not pray for an easy life, pray for the strength to endure a difficult one." Sometimes, anger can be a powerful motivator that propels us forward and gives us the strength we need to tackle challenges head-on. So don't be afraid to tap into your anger when you need to.

Of course, anger can also be destructive if not channeled properly. As Eleanor Roosevelt once said, "Anger is like a thorn in the heart...the tree is healthy, but the fruit is bitter." So while it's important to use anger as a tool to motivate you, it's also important to keep it in check and make sure it doesn't consume you.

When you feel that rage building inside of you, it's important to channel it in a positive direction. As author Brené Brown puts it, "I define vulnerability as emotional risk, exposure, uncertainty. It fuels our daily lives. And I've come to the belief...that vulnerability is our most accurate measure of courage." By using your anger to take risks and push yourself out of your comfort zone, you can tap into your courage and make positive changes in your life.

That being said, it's also important not to let your anger take over completely. As the ancient philosopher Aristotle once said, "Anybody can become angry - that is easy, but to be angry with the right person and to the right degree and at the right time and for the right purpose, and in the right way - that is not within everybody's power and is not easy." So make sure you're directing your anger towards the right things, and in a way that is productive rather than destructive.

When you're feeling angry, it can be tempting to lash out at others. But as Mahatma Gandhi famously said, "An eye for an eye will only make the whole world blind." So instead of seeking revenge or retribution, try to channel your anger into something positive, whether it's working towards a goal, speaking up for what you believe in, or simply using that energy to propel yourself forward.

Of course, it's not always easy to know what to do with our anger. As the author and speaker Elizabeth Gilbert puts it, "We don't know how to deal with it because we've been raised in a culture that says, 'Just don't get angry.' It's like saying, 'Just don't get hungry.' It's a natural human emotion." So if you're feeling angry, don't try to suppress it - instead, try to figure out how you can use it to your advantage.

One way to do this is by using your anger to push yourself to new heights. As basketball player Michael Jordan once said, "I've missed more than 9,000 shots in my career. I've lost almost 300 games. 26 times I've been trusted to take the game-winning shot and missed. I've failed over and over and over again in my life. And that is why I succeed." By using your anger as fuel for your ambitions, you can turn setbacks and failures into opportunities for growth and success.

It's important to remember that anger is just one emotion among many. As the Dalai Lama once said, "Anger, hatred, and jealousy never solve problems, only affection, concern, and respect can do that." So while anger can be a useful tool, it's important not to let it blind us to the other emotions that are just as important.

Ultimately, getting angry can be a transformative experience that leads to positive change in your life. As the writer James Baldwin once said, "Not everything that is faced can be changed, but nothing can be changed until it is faced."

So the next time you're feeling stuck or complacent, try getting angry with yourself and your circumstances. Use that anger as fuel to propel yourself towards your goals and make the changes you need to live your best life. As the saying goes, "Well-behaved women (and men) seldom make history."

CHAPTER 12

WHY BEING WOKE CAN DESTROY ESSENTIALISM

Today, people hide behind a lot of anomalies in the name of being woke. What they end up doing is sacrificing common sense, values and sense of being on the alter of alternate freedom. Something is largely amiss in today's world and no one is brave enough to question it, why - interests. These interests may look large today, tomorrow or when you choose to switch favours.

Being woke is like wearing a pair of glasses with only one lens. You might see the world in a new way, but you're missing half the picture. Essentialism, the belief that there are inherent differences between groups of people, has been a cornerstone of our understanding of society for centuries. While it's important to acknowledge these differences, we must also recognize that they do not define us.

Imagine going to a restaurant and ordering a dish without knowing what it's made of. That's what being woke is like - you're so focused on the message that you forget to examine the substance. Essentialism, on the other hand, encourages us to understand the underlying factors that make us who we are.

For some people, their newfound sense of purpose can be like being stuck in a never-ending cycle of outrage. You're constantly reacting to the latest controversy or social media post, without taking the time to reflect on your own values and beliefs. Essentialism encourages us to take a step back and examine what's truly important to us.

It's like going to a party and only talking to people who look and think like you. Sure, you might feel comfortable in that echo chamber, but you're missing out on the richness and diversity of human experience. Essentialism encourages us to embrace our differences and learn from one another.

Being woke is like trying to navigate a new city without a map. You might stumble upon some interesting sights, but you're also likely to get lost and miss out on some key destinations. Essentialism provides us with a framework for understanding our place in society and how we relate to others.

The puzzle is, you might be able to piece together some of the picture, but it will never be complete. Essentialism gives us a complete picture of who we are as individuals and as members of society.

You must be honest with yourself, are you really woke or seemingly part of a maddening that has no end game.

CHAPTER 13

CHALLENGES ARE BRICKS

Challenges are tough; they are the modern psychological bricks that builds the dynasty we desire. If well cemented by tolerance and courage, they hold firm the units of out mental elasticity.

"Challenges are what make life interesting and overcoming them is what makes life meaningful." - Joshua J. Marine

Life can be tough. There's no denying it. We all face challenges and obstacles in our daily lives, some bigger than others. But the way we approach these challenges is what truly defines us. We can choose to let them defeat us, or we can use them as building bricks to create something stronger and better.

Think of challenges like puzzle pieces. Individually, they may seem daunting and overwhelming, but when put together, they can create a beautiful and complete picture. It's the same with challenges in life. Each one may be difficult to overcome on its own, but when we use them as building bricks, we can create a life that is strong and resilient.

One of the greatest examples of this is the story of J.K. Rowling. Before she became a household name with her Harry Potter series, she faced incredible challenges. She was a single mother living on welfare, struggling to make ends meet. But instead of letting her circumstances defeat her, she used them as building bricks. She wrote her first book in cafes while her baby slept, never giving up on her dream of becoming a writer. And now, she is one of the most successful authors of all time.

"Success is not final, failure is not fatal: it is the courage to continue that counts." - Winston Churchill

Another example is the story of Thomas Edison. He failed over a thousand times before he finally invented the light bulb. But instead of giving up, he used each failure as a building brick, learning from his mistakes and trying again. Without his persistence, we may never have had one of the most important inventions of modern times.

"Challenges are gifts that force us to search for a new center of gravity. Don't fight them. Just find a new way to stand." - Oprah Winfrey

But it's not just famous people who can use challenges as building bricks. Every one of us faces our own unique challenges in life, and we all have the ability to turn them into something positive. Whether it's a difficult job, a relationship problem, or a health issue, we can choose to let it defeat us, or we can use it to make us stronger.

One of the keys to using challenges as building bricks is to have a growth mindset. This means seeing challenges as opportunities for growth and learning, rather than as threats or obstacles. It means embracing the discomfort that comes with challenges and using it to fuel our progress.

"Challenges are what make life interesting and overcoming them is what makes life meaningful." - Joshua J. Marine

Of course, it's not always easy to have a growth mindset. Sometimes it takes practice and effort to shift our perspective. But the more we practice, the easier it becomes. And the more we use challenges as building bricks, the stronger and more resilient we become.

"Believe you can and you're halfway there." - Theodore Roosevelt

So, the next time you face a challenge in your life, remember that it's an opportunity to use it as a building brick. Embrace the discomfort, learn from your mistakes, and keep moving forward. You may just surprise yourself with what you can create. As the great Maya Angelou once said, "I can be changed by what happens to me. But I refuse to be reduced by it." Let challenges be the building bricks that create a better you.

CHAPTER 14

THE BURDEN OF GREED

There is no satisfaction being greedy, you always want what you don't need. Greedy kills the appetite for common good and leaves a huge chasm in the ground. Greedy people don't see past themselves, like caterpillars, they annihilate everything on their path.

Greed is an insatiable desire to acquire more wealth, power, or status, beyond what one needs or deserves. It is a destructive trait that undermines the moral fiber of society and corrodes the spirit of human generosity and empathy. Greed has been responsible for some of the worst atrocities in history, from the slave trade to colonialism, to the exploitation of natural resources and the environment. It is a burden that we all must bear, but one that we can overcome with a concerted effort to promote ethical and responsible behavior.

One of the most striking examples of the burden of greed is the case of the Ogoni people of Nigeria. The Ogoni people are a minority group in Nigeria who have been exploited for their oil resources for decades. Despite being one of the wealthiest regions in Nigeria, the Ogoni people remain impoverished, with high rates of infant mortality, malnutrition, and unemployment. The oil companies have exploited their resources, destroyed their environment, and left them with no means of sustenance.

One of the most prominent Ogoni activists was Ken Saro-Wiwa, who fought tirelessly to defend the rights of his people and to expose the corrupt practices of the oil companies. In his book, "A Month and a Day," Saro-Wiwa wrote, "Greed and corruption have become so ingrained in our society that it has become a way of life." He argued that the Nigerian government and the oil companies were responsible for the poverty and environmental degradation that had devastated the Ogoni people. Saro-Wiwa was eventually executed by the Nigerian government for his activism, but his legacy lives on as a symbol of resistance against greed and oppression.

Another example of the burden of greed is the case of the 419 scam, also known as the Nigerian Prince scam. This is a fraudulent scheme that has become synonymous with Nigeria, in which scammers promise to transfer a large sum of money to their victims in exchange for a small fee. The scam has been so successful that it has become a cliché, and has even been parodied in popular culture.

The 419 scam is a manifestation of the greed and desperation that many Nigerians face. It is a symptom of a society in which wealth is concentrated in the hands of a few, and opportunities for social mobility are scarce. The scammers prey on the vulnerability and gullibility of their victims, but they too are victims of a system that has failed them.

In a speech to the United Nations General Assembly in 1984, Nigerian writer Chinua Achebe spoke of the impact of greed on Nigerian society. He said, "The problem with Nigeria is simply and squarely a failure of leadership. There is nothing wrong with the Nigerian character. There is nothing wrong with the Nigerian land or climate or water or air or anything else. The Nigerian problem is the unwillingness or inability of its leaders to rise to the responsibility, to the challenge of personal example which are the hallmarks of true leadership."

Achebe's words are a call to action for all Nigerians to rise up against the burden of greed and corruption that has plagued their society for too long. It is a challenge to take responsibility for their own actions and to demand accountability from their leaders. It is a reminder that the burden of greed is not an individual problem, but a collective one, that requires a collective effort to overcome.

One of the most inspiring stories of overcoming the burden of greed in Nigeria is the story of Mohammed Yunus. Yunus is a Bangladeshi economist and social entrepreneur who founded the Grameen Bank, which provides microfinance loans to poor people, particularly women, in Bangladesh. Yunus believes that poverty is not a result of individual failure, but of systemic failure, and that the best way to combat poverty

The burden of greed is not unique to Nigeria, but is a global issue that affects all societies to some extent. In many parts of the world, wealth inequality has reached unprecedented levels, with small elite holding the majority of the world's wealth and resources, while the majority of people struggle to make ends meet. This has resulted in a myriad of social and economic problems, including poverty, hunger, environmental degradation, and political instability.

One of the most striking examples of the global burden of greed is the exploitation of natural resources in developing countries. Many multinational corporations and wealthy individuals from developed countries have exploited the natural resources of developing countries, often with the collusion of corrupt governments, in order to enrich themselves at the expense of local communities.

For example, in the Amazon rainforest, indigenous communities are fighting against large-scale mining and logging operations that are destroying their homes and livelihoods. In the Congo, the mining of minerals used in electronics has fueled a conflict that has claimed millions of lives and caused widespread human suffering. In the Arctic, the rush for oil and gas has threatened the fragile ecosystem and the way of life of indigenous peoples.

The burden of greed is also evident in the way in which wealthy individuals and corporations use their power to influence politics and shape policies to their advantage. This has resulted in a political system that is increasingly dominated by a small elite, who use their wealth to advance their interests at the expense of the common good. This has led to a growing sense of disillusionment and anger among ordinary people, who feel that their voices are not being heard and that the system is rigged against them.

The COVID-19 pandemic has also highlighted the burden of greed in the global response to the crisis. The unequal distribution of vaccines, with wealthy countries hoarding doses while poor countries struggle to vaccinate their populations, is a stark example of how greed and self-interest can undermine global efforts to combat a common threat.

This has not only resulted in unnecessary suffering and death but also threatens to prolong the pandemic and its economic and social impacts.

Despite these challenges, there are also many examples of individuals and communities working together to overcome the burden of greed and promote a more just and sustainable world. From the rise of the sharing economy to the growth of social enterprises and impact investing, there are many innovative solutions being developed to address some of the world's most pressing problems.

In conclusion, the burden of greed is a global issue that requires a collective effort to overcome. It is a challenge to our moral values and our ability to work together for the common good. While it may seem overwhelming at times, we must not lose sight of the fact that we all have a role to play in creating a better world, one that is more just, equitable, and sustainable.

CHAPTER 15

PASSION KEEPS YOU GOING

When monotomy lords your everyday activity, passion helps you find Rhythm. For decades, great minds have laid emphasis on far passion got them, it's hardly for the financial gratification but the entirety of fulfilment. Passion heralds the extent you would go if you keep your energy levels up and enjoy what makes you happy in the doing - primarily.

Passion is the fuel that keeps us going; it's what pushes us to achieve our goals, and to overcome obstacles that would otherwise hinder our progress. Without passion, our lives would be dull and unfulfilled, and we would be resigned to living a life of mediocrity. But with passion, we can accomplish great things, and we can make a real difference in the world.

Now, when it comes to passion, there are a few things that we need to keep in mind. First and foremost, passion is not something that can be forced. You can't just decide to be passionate about something and expect it to stick. Passion is something that comes from within, and it's something that needs to be nurtured and developed over time.

But once you do find your passion, it's important to hold onto it with everything you've got. Because passion is what separates the people who succeed from the people who don't. It's what drives us to go the extra mile, to put in the extra effort, and to push ourselves beyond our limits.

Here are some tips on how to go about finding your passion. First and foremost, you need to try new things. Get out of your comfort zone and try something that you've never done before. Who knows, you might just discover that you have a hidden talent that you never knew about.

Another thing you can do is think back to your childhood. What did you enjoy doing when you were a kid? Did you love to draw? Play music? Write stories? Those things that you loved as a child could be a clue to your passion.

Don't be afraid to ask for help. Talk to your friends and family, ask them what they think your passion is. Sometimes, other people can see things in us that we can't see ourselves.

Now, I know that finding your passion is not always easy. But trust me when I say that it's worth it. Because once you find your passion, you'll be unstoppable. You'll have a fire in your belly that will keep you going no matter what.

Passion is not just about finding something that you enjoy doing. It's about finding something that you're willing to work for, something that you're willing to fight for. Because let's face it, nothing worth having comes easy.

In the words of the great Nigerian author Chimamanda Ngozi Adichie, "Passion is not merely a hobby. It is a force that unlocks creativity, imagination and innovation. It is the willingness to persevere through the difficult times and the ability to stay motivated when the going gets tough."

And that's exactly what passion is all about. It's about being willing to put in the work, even when it's hard. Because when you're truly passionate about something, the hard work doesn't feel like work at all. It feels like a labour of love.

Now, let me give you an example. Take the Nigerian music industry, for instance. There are countless musicians in Nigeria who are passionate about what they do. They spend countless hours in the studio, perfecting their craft. They perform at gigs all around the country, sometimes for little or no pay. They do it because they love it. They do it because they're passionate about their music.

Nigerian music is just one example of how passion can drive success. There are countless other examples, both in Africa and around the world.

Take Elon Musk, for instance. The billionaire entrepreneur is passionate about space exploration and the future of technology. He spends countless hours working on projects like SpaceX and Tesla, pushing the boundaries of what's possible and inspiring a new generation of innovators.

Or look at Malala Yousafzai, the Pakistani activist who became a global icon for her advocacy of girls' education. She risked her life to speak out against the Taliban and fight for the rights of girls in her country. Her passion and dedication to the cause inspired millions around the world and earned her a Nobel Peace Prize.

And then there's Oprah Winfrey, the media mogul who overcame a difficult childhood to become one of the most successful and influential women in the world. She is passionate about storytelling and using her platform to inspire and uplift others. Her passion has led her to create an empire that includes television shows, magazines, and a network that reaches millions of people around the world.

These are just a few examples, but the truth is that passion is a driving force behind countless success stories, both big and small.

In conclusion, passion is not just a fluffy buzzword or a feel-good sentiment. It's a powerful force that can drive us to achieve great things and make a real difference in the world. Whether it's Nigerian music, space exploration, girls' education, or any other pursuit, passion is what separates the ordinary from the extraordinary. So if you haven't found your passion yet, don't give up. Keep trying new things, keep pushing yourself, and keep searching until you find that thing that sets your soul on fire.

CHAPTER 16

TAKE THAT RISK!

Life is worth living with risks - let that sink in!

Living is an adventure propounded by risks and those who make discoveries do so taking risks. It can go either ways, but then, what the hell! hell, it could go your way!

You can choose not to gamble your money in casinos or related ventures, but you can gamble your hunch by taking your chance at something great and defining.

Taking risks is a fundamental part of life. From the moment we are born, we are constantly faced with challenges and opportunities that require us to make decisions and take action. Whether it's starting a new business, pursuing a new career path, or even just trying a new hobby, taking risks can lead to some of the most rewarding experiences in life.

However, many people are often afraid of taking risks. They may fear failure, rejection, or the unknown, and as a result, they may miss out on opportunities for growth and personal development. In this motivation, we will explore the importance of taking risks, the benefits it can bring, and how to overcome the fear that often holds us back.

One of the main benefits of taking risks is that it can lead to personal growth and development. When we take risks, we are often forced to step outside of our comfort zones and confront our fears and insecurities. This can be a scary and challenging process, but it can also be incredibly rewarding. By facing our fears and overcoming obstacles, we can develop resilience, self-confidence, and a sense of accomplishment.

For example, think about someone who has always dreamed of starting their own business but has been too afraid to take the leap. By taking the risk and starting their own business, they may encounter challenges such as financial uncertainty, competition, and a steep learning curve. However, by persevering through these challenges and finding ways to overcome them, they can develop valuable skills and knowledge that can benefit them in many areas of life.

In addition to personal growth, taking risks can also lead to great rewards. Whether it's financial success, career advancement, or personal fulfillment, taking risks can open up new opportunities that may have otherwise been inaccessible. Of course, there is always the possibility of failure, but the potential for success can often outweigh the risks.

Consider the story of J.K. Rowling, the author of the Harry Potter series. When she first began writing the series, she faced multiple rejections from publishers and struggled with financial instability. However, she persevered and continued to take risks by submitting her manuscript to more publishers, eventually leading to the success of one of the best-selling book series of all time.

It's important to note that taking risks doesn't always have to involve grand gestures or life-changing decisions. Even small risks, such as trying a new food or engaging in a new social activity, can lead to positive outcomes and personal growth.

However, despite the potential benefits of taking risks, many people are still held back by fear. Fear of failure, fear of rejection, and fear of the unknown are all common reasons why people may be hesitant to take risks. Overcoming these fears is essential in order to fully embrace the opportunities that taking risks can bring.

One way to overcome fear is to reframe the way we think about failure. Rather than viewing failure as a negative outcome, we can instead see it as an opportunity for growth and learning. Failure can be a valuable experience that teaches us important lessons and helps us to become more resilient and adaptable.

As the famous inventor Thomas Edison once said, "I have not failed. I've just found 10,000 ways that won't work." This attitude of perseverance and resilience is a key factor in overcoming the fear of failure and taking risks.

Another way to overcome fear is to practice mindfulness and focus on the present moment. When we are anxious about the future or dwelling on past mistakes, it can be difficult to take action and move forward. By practicing mindfulness and focusing on the present moment, we can reduce anxiety and cultivate a sense of calm and clarity that can help us make more informed and confident decisions.

Real-life examples of taking risks can be found in all areas of society. From entrepreneurs who start their own businesses to athletes who push their bodies to the limit

CHAPTER 17

EXPOSURE GETS YOU AHEAD

Exposure is everything; it is the currency of learning. New things enlarge your horizon and makes you a complete fit of a man. Travelling, meeting new people, drifting into new conversations will only help you get ahead and understand how the world is involving. In other words, take the joy to learn new things.

Exposure, in simple terms, means making something visible to the world. It can be a person, an idea, a product, or even a cause. Exposure is an important aspect of success because it creates awareness and visibility, which can lead to opportunities and growth. In today's fast-paced world, where competition is fierce, exposure is the key to getting ahead. In this article, we will explore how exposure can lead to success and share examples, anecdotes, and popular quotes that will inspire and provoke thought.

Exposure is the key to unlocking success in every aspect of life. Whether it's in the professional or personal realm, exposing oneself to new experiences, ideas, and people is crucial for growth and advancement. Exposure allows us to learn, evolve, and develop new skills that can help us excel in our careers and personal lives. In this essay, we will explore the power of exposure and how it can get us ahead in life.

One of the most common ways that exposure can get us ahead is by expanding our networks. Meeting new people from different backgrounds, industries, and experiences can lead to opportunities that we may not have had otherwise. Whether it's finding a new job, a mentor, or a business partner, the more people we meet, the more doors will open for us. As the saying goes, "your network is your net worth," and exposure can help us build a valuable network that can pay off in the long run.

A prime example of this is the story of how Oprah Winfrey got her start in the media industry. As a young journalist, Oprah moved to Baltimore to co-anchor the evening news. While working in Baltimore, she was exposed to a whole new world of media and entertainment. She took on new roles, such as hosting a local talk show, and gained exposure to new audiences. This exposure eventually led to her being discovered by a national network and ultimately becoming the media mogul that we know today. Oprah's exposure to new opportunities and people was a key factor in her success.

When we expose ourselves to different cultures, beliefs, and experiences, we become more open-minded and empathetic. This can help us become better problem-solvers and communicators, as we are able to see issues from multiple angles. It can also help us connect with people on a deeper level, as we are able to relate to their experiences and understand their perspectives.

Exposure can be achieved in different ways, such as through social media, networking, public speaking, or even taking risks. The more exposure a person or a thing gets, the more likely they are to be noticed and remembered. Exposure can lead to recognition, which can result in opportunities for growth and success. For instance, a small business that has a strong online presence through social media and other marketing efforts is more likely to attract new customers and expand its reach than a business that operates solely in its local area.

One example of this is the story of Anthony Bourdain, the late chef and travel writer. Bourdain was known for his love of exploring different cultures through food and travel. His exposure to new cultures and people not only made him a better chef and writer but also a more compassionate and empathetic human being. In his book, "Kitchen Confidential," Bourdain writes, "Travel isn't always pretty. It isn't always comfortable. Sometimes it hurts, it even breaks your heart. But that's okay. The journey changes you; it should change you. It leaves marks on your memory, on your consciousness, on your heart, and on your body. You take something with you. Hopefully, you leave something good behind."

Exposure can also help us develop new skills and knowledge that can advance our careers. When we expose ourselves to new industries, technologies, and ideas, we are able to learn and adapt to new challenges. This can make us more marketable in the job market and give us a competitive edge over our peers.

CHAPTER 18

UPDATE YOUR TALENT

The world is filled with millions of talents, some doing the same thing, others scaling the 'wow' perimeters. This means to be a step further, one must push the boundaries of one's talent. There is a pressing demand to update what you to make a global statement if you treasure one.

In today's fast-paced world, updating your talent is crucial to stay relevant in your field of work. The world is constantly evolving, and technology is advancing at a rapid pace. To remain competitive, it's important to upgrade your skills and knowledge base constantly. If you are not continually updating your talent, you risk becoming obsolete.

Updating your talent can take on many different forms. It may involve learning new skills, taking courses, attending workshops, networking, or gaining experience in different areas. Whatever form it takes, it requires a commitment to continuous learning.

There are many benefits to updating your talent. It can enhance your career prospects, increase your earning potential, and give you a competitive advantage in your field. Additionally, it can boost your confidence, increase your job satisfaction, and help you stay engaged and interested in your work.

One of the best examples of the importance of updating your talent is the music industry. In this industry, musicians who fail to evolve and update their talent often fall behind the times and become less relevant. They are quickly replaced by newer, fresher talent. One such example is Madonna, who has managed to stay relevant for decades by constantly reinventing herself and updating her musical style.

Similarly, in the business world, updating your talent can be the difference between success and failure. According to Forbes, "The key to staying ahead in business is to constantly update your talent, which includes acquiring new skills and competencies."

The rapid pace of technological change has made updating your talent even more critical. The World Economic Forum predicts that by 2025, over half of all employees will need to update their skillsets to remain employable. The same report suggests that by 2030, over one billion people will need to learn new skills to keep up with the changing job market.

The importance of updating your talent is not limited to the professional world. It's also essential for personal growth and development. Learning new skills and gaining knowledge can help you broaden your perspective, increase your creativity, and make you a more interesting and well-rounded person.

There are many ways to update your talent. You may consider taking online courses or attending workshops in your field. You can also network with other professionals to gain new insights and perspectives. Additionally, you may want to consider volunteering or taking on new projects at work to gain experience in different areas.

One example of the benefits of updating your talent is the success story of LinkedIn CEO Jeff Weiner. In an interview with the New York Times, Weiner credits his success to his commitment to continuous learning. He stated, "I have a belief that if you're not learning, you're falling behind. And if you're falling behind, you're becoming obsolete."

Another example is the story of entrepreneur and author Tim Ferriss, who emphasizes the importance of updating your talent in his book "The 4-Hour Work Week." Ferriss suggests that updating your talent is essential for achieving success in today's economy. He writes, "The most important skill to develop is the ability to learn quickly and effectively. If you can do that, you'll be able to stay ahead of the curve and succeed in virtually any field."

It's essential for professional success, personal growth, and remaining relevant in your field of work. The benefits of updating your talent are numerous, including enhanced career prospects, increased earning potential, and a competitive advantage. To stay ahead of the curve, you must be committed to continuous learning and updating your skillset. As Madonna said, "I'm tough, I'm ambitious, and I know exactly what I want. If that makes me a bitch, okay."

CHAPTER 19

PROVE YOURSELF

There is no limit to what you can do or achieve but first you must prove yourself worthy. It may be by acquiring more knowledge, learning a skill, getting to know certain people, leaving your comfort zone - prove that you are worthy of the prize you seek.

Proving oneself is a challenge that many people face throughout their lives, whether in personal or professional settings. It can be daunting to take on new challenges and push oneself outside of one's comfort zone, but the rewards can be significant in terms of personal growth, career success, and self-confidence. In this essay, I will explore the theme of proving oneself through a selection of quotes and examples from Africa, Europe, and the United States.

In Africa, there are many inspiring stories of individuals who have overcome adversity and proven themselves in the face of great challenges. One example is Nelson Mandela, who spent 27 years in prison for his role in the struggle against apartheid in South Africa. After his release, Mandela became the country's first black president and worked tirelessly to promote reconciliation and unity in a deeply divided society. He once said, "I learned that courage was not the absence of fear, but the triumph over it. The brave man is not he who does not feel afraid, but he who conquers that fear."

Another inspiring figure from Africa is Wangari Maathai, the Kenyan environmental and political activist who became the first African woman to win the Nobel Peace Prize. Maathai founded the Green Belt Movement, which focused on empowering rural women to plant trees and restore degraded land. She once said, "You cannot enslave a mind that knows itself. That values itself. That understands itself."

In Europe, there are also many examples of individuals who have proven themselves through their achievements and perseverance. One such example is Marie Curie, the Polish-born physicist and chemist who was the first woman to win a Nobel Prize and the first person to win two Nobel Prizes in different fields. Curie once said, "Life is not easy for any of us. But what of that? We must have perseverance and, above all, confidence in ourselves. We must believe that we are gifted for something and that this thing must be attained."

Another inspiring figure from Europe is Malala Yousafzai, the Pakistani activist for girls' education who survived a Taliban assassination attempt and went on to become the youngest-ever Nobel laureate. Yousafzai once said, "One child, one teacher, one book, one pen can change the world. Education is the only solution. Education first."

In the United States, there are countless examples of individuals who have overcome obstacles and proven themselves through their hard work and dedication. One such example is Oprah Winfrey, the media mogul who rose from poverty and abuse to become one of the most influential and successful women in the world. Winfrey once said, "I believe that every single event in life happens in an opportunity to choose love over fear."

Another inspiring figure from the United States is Barack Obama, the country's first black president who overcame racial barriers and became a symbol of hope and change for millions of people around the world. Obama once said, "Change will not come if we wait for some other person or some other time. We are the ones we've been waiting for. We are the change that we seek."

These examples from Africa, Europe, and the United States show that proving oneself is not just a matter of talent or ability, but also of determination, perseverance, and courage. It requires taking risks and facing one's fears, but the rewards can be tremendous in terms of personal growth, career success, and self-confidence. Whether it is overcoming discrimination, fighting for social justice, or pursuing a dream, the key is to believe in oneself and one's abilities.

Proving oneself is a universal one that transcends geographical and cultural boundaries. It is a challenge that we all face at some point in our lives, but it is also an opportunity to grow and learn.

CHAPTER 20

TAKE THAT OPPORTUNITY NOW

Opportunity is no longer recumbent or one that comes knocking, sometimes you have to approach it and grab it, but, like the boys scout motto - you must be prepared. There is a piece of you that completes today's puzzle.

Opportunities come in many different forms and present themselves at various times throughout our lives. They can be the chance to pursue a new career, travel to a foreign country, or start a new relationship. Sometimes, we may not even recognize an opportunity when it arises, and it passes us by without us even realizing it. However, it is important to take advantage of opportunities when they come because they can lead to life-changing experiences and personal growth. In this motivation, we will explore why it is important to seize opportunities when they present themselves, provide examples of individuals who did just that, and offer practical tips for identifying and taking advantage of opportunities.

Taking opportunities can lead to personal growth and development, providing us with the chance to challenge ourselves and expand our horizons. When we take opportunities, we expose ourselves to new experiences, perspectives, and challenges and we learn from these experiences. In turn, this learning can lead to personal growth and development, helping us to become more resilient, adaptable, and confident.

Opportunities can also help us achieve our goals and aspirations. For example, if we have always dreamed of starting our own business, taking an opportunity to attend a networking event or meeting with a mentor can provide us with valuable insights and connections that can help us achieve our goal. Similarly, if we want to pursue a career in a particular field, taking opportunities to gain experience and build our skills can help us achieve success.

Perhaps most importantly, taking opportunities can lead to happiness and fulfillment. When we pursue our passions and interests, we feel a sense of purpose and satisfaction. Taking opportunities allows us to explore new interests and passions, and can help us discover what we truly love to do. This can lead to a sense of fulfillment and happiness that cannot be found in material possessions or superficial achievements.

Here is a list of persons who took their opportunities and became a global household name:

J.K. Rowling - author of the Harry Potter series

Thomas Edison - inventor of the light bulb and phonograph

Oprah Winfrey - media mogul and philanthropist

Elon Musk - entrepreneur and founder of Tesla, SpaceX, and PayPal

Steve Jobs - co-founder of Apple Inc.

Mark Zuckerberg - co-founder of Facebook

Serena Williams - tennis player and entrepreneur

Richard Branson - founder of Virgin Group

Bill Gates - co-founder of Microsoft

Beyoncé - singer and actress

Walt Disney - founder of The Walt Disney Company

Arianna Huffington - founder of The Huffington Post

Michael Jordan - basketball player and entrepreneur

Larry Page - co-founder of Google

Jeff Bezos - founder of Amazon

Warren Buffett - investor and philanthropist

Maya Angelou - writer and civil rights activist

Michelle Obama - former First Lady of the United States

Cristiano Ronaldo - soccer player and entrepreneur

Henry Ford - founder of Ford Motor Company

Nelson Mandela - anti-apartheid revolutionary and former President of South Africa

Stephen Hawking - physicist and author

Simone Biles - gymnast and activist

Kamala Harris - Vice President of the United States

Martin Luther King Jr. - civil rights activist

Malala Yousafzai - education activist and Nobel Peace Prize winner

Barack Obama - former President of the United States

Ellen DeGeneres - comedian and talk show host

Jackie Chan - actor and martial artist

Vincent van Gogh - artist

Madonna - singer and actress

Jane Goodall - primatologist and conservationist

Tiger Woods - golfer and entrepreneur

Anne Frank - writer and Holocaust victim

Billie Jean King - tennis player and activist

Jerry Seinfeld - comedian and actor

Celine Dion - singer

Bruce Lee - martial artist and actor

Dalai Lama - spiritual leader of Tibet

Greta Thunberg - climate change activist

Lebron James - basketball player and entrepreneur

Mahatma Gandhi - political and spiritual leader of India

Serena Williams - tennis player and entrepreneur

Michael Phelps - swimmer and Olympic gold medalist

William Shakespeare - playwright and poet

Nelson Rockefeller - former Vice President of the United States

Hillary Clinton - former Secretary of State of the United States

Margaret Thatcher - former Prime Minister of the United Kingdom

Winston Churchill - former Prime Minister of the United Kingdom

PRACTICAL TIPS FOR TAKING OPPORTUNITIES

While it is important to take opportunities when they come, it can sometimes be difficult to recognize them. Here are some practical tips for identifying and taking advantage of opportunities:

Keep an open mind: Opportunities can come from unexpected places, so it is important to keep an open mind and be willing to explore new experiences and ideas.

Network: Building relationships with others can help us identify and take advantage of opportunities. Attend networking events, join professional organizations, and connect with others on social media.

Be proactive: Sometimes, we need to create our own opportunities. Take the initiative to seek out new experiences and opportunities that align with your goals and interests.

REFERENCES

"Sangfroid: Calm in the Face of Adversity" - Psychology Today

"The Upside of Weakness" by Brené Brown:

Gladwell, Malcolm. "The Naked Face." The New Yorker, August 5, 2002. https://www.newyorker.com/magazine

Lerner, Michele. "Why You Shouldn't Always Trust Your Gut." Forbes, September 16, 2019. https://www.forbes.com/sites/michelelerner/2019/09/16/why-you-shouldnt-always-trust-your-gut/?sh=3d3cf3d0196b.

Weiner, J. (2014). LinkedIn's CEO on the Importance of 'Learning in the Flow of Work'. The New York Times. https://www.nytimes.com/2014/04/06/business/linkedin-ceo-jeff-weiner-on-the-importance-of-learning-in-the-flow-of-work.html.

Ferriss, T. (2007). The 4-Hour Work Week: Escape 9-5, Live Anywhere, and Join the New Rich. Crown Publishing Group.

Madonna. (n.d.). BrainyQuote.

McGregor, Jena. "Why You Shouldn't Always Trust Your Instincts." The Washington Post, July 22, 2015. https://www.washingtonpost.com/news/on-leadership/wp/2015/07/22/why-you-shouldnt-always-trust-your-instincts/.

Moynihan, Michael. "Don't Trust the Crowd: How the Wisdom of Crowds Can Foul Your Judgment." American Psychological Association, February 2017. https://www.apa.org/monitor/2017/02/cover-crowd.

Sunstein, Cass R. "The Perils of Groupthink." The New Yorker, January 8, 2015. https://www.newyorker.com/news/daily-comment/the-perils-of-groupthink.

Tversky, Amos, and Daniel Kahneman. "Judgment under Uncertainty: Heuristics and Biases." Science 185, no.

Nussbaum, M. (2016). Anger and forgiveness: Resentment, generosity, justice. Oxford University Press.

Gay, R. (2018). Not that bad: Dispatches from rape culture. HarperCollins.

Greenwald, G. (2013). With liberty and justice for some: How the law is used to destroy equality and protect the powerful. Metropolitan Books.

Pinker, S. (2018). Enlightenment now: The case for reason, science, humanism, and progress. Penguin.

Kahan, D. M., Peters, E., Dawson, E. C., & Slovic, P. (2017). Motivated numeracy and enlightened self-government. Behavioral Science & Policy, 3(1), 26-39.

Tetlock, P. E., & Mitchell, G. (2015). The right and wrong way to forecast political outcomes. In Expert political judgment: How good is it? How can we know? (pp. 25-55). Princeton University Press.

Sunstein, C. R. (2009). Going to extremes: How like minds unite and divide. Oxford University Press.

Kahneman, D. (2011). Thinking, fast and slow. Macmillan.

Tajfel, H. (1982). Social identity and intergroup relations. Cambridge University Press.

Haidt, J. (2013). The righteous mind: Why good people are divided by politics and religion. Vintage.

Okonofua, B. (2019). Nigerian Music and Globalisation: The Rise of Afrobeats. Journal of African Cultural Studies, 31(2), 211-225. https://doi.org/10.1080/13696815.2018.1494995

Biagi, S. (2020). Elon Musk: The Rise of SpaceX and Tesla. FOCUS Quarterly, 1(1), 29-36. https://doi.org/10.15379/2410-3329.2020.01.02

Yousafzai, M., & Lamb, C. (2013). I Am Malala: The Girl Who Stood Up for Education and Was Shot by the Taliban. Little, Brown and Company.

Winfrey, O. (2014). What I Know For Sure. Flatiron Books.

Grant, A. M., & Dweck, C. S. (2003). Clarifying achievement goals and their impact. Journal of Personality and Social Psychology, 85(3), 541-553.

Bandura, A. (1997). Self-efficacy: The exercise of control. New York: W.H. Freeman and Company.

Seligman, M. E., & Csikszentmihalyi, M. (2014). Positive psychology: An introduction. Springer.

Duckworth, A. L., Peterson, C., Matthews, M. D., & Kelly, D. R. (2007). Grit: Perseverance and passion for long-term goals. Journal of Personality and Social Psychology, 92(6), 1087-1101.

McGrath, J. (2017, November 16). Oprah Winfrey: The journey to media mogul. BBC News. Retrieved March 31, 2023, from https://www.bbc.com/news/entertainment-arts-42014079

Bourdain, A. (2007). Kitchen Confidential: Adventures in the Culinary Underbelly. Harper Perennial.

LaRoche, J. (2018, November 13). Elon Musk's Career Path to CEO of Tesla and SpaceX. Investopedia. Retrieved March 31, 2023

Oxfam. (2020). Time to Care: Unpaid and underpaid care work and the global inequality crisis.

Retrieved from https://www.oxfam.org/en/research/time-care

The Guardian. (2021). Covid vaccine inequality threatens to prolong pandemic, says Red Cross chief. Retrieved from https://www.theguardian.com/world/2021/feb/17/covid-vaccine-inequality-threatens-to-prolong-pandemic-says-red-cross-chief

Human Rights Watch. (2021). DR Congo: Abuses in Chinese-Owned Mines. Retrieved from https://www.hrw.org/news/2021/02/04/dr-congo-abuses-chinese-owned-mines

Mandela, Nelson. Long Walk to Freedom: The Autobiography of Nelson Mandela. Back Bay Books, 1995.

Maathai, Wangari. Unbowed: A Memoir. Anchor Books, 2007.

Curie, Marie. Pierre Curie. Dover Publications, 1965.

Yousafzai, Malala. I Am Malala: The Girl Who Stood Up for Education and Was Shot by the Taliban. Little, Brown and Company, 2013.

The Power of Taking Risks" by Michael Hyatt - This article explores the importance of taking risks and seizing opportunities in order to achieve success.

"The Art of Seizing Opportunities" by Jane Wesman - This article provides tips and strategies for recognizing and taking advantage of opportunities.

ABOUT THE AUTHOR

Meet Fortune Omosola, the vibrant author behind the mesmerizing book, 'The Nuances of Poetry.' With over a decade of experience in digital broadcast journalism, Fortune has left an indelible mark on the world of TV, radio and online journalism. As a seasoned news reporter, editor and on-air personality, his work is nothing short of exceptional.

But that's not all. Fortune is a true creative at heart, with a passion for spoken word and voice over artistry. He brings a unique perspective to his writing, infusing his work with his incredible talent and captivating storytelling.

He has a couple of poetry works and motivations published on Amazon.

With an unwavering dedication to his craft and a talent that knows no bounds, Fortune Omosola is a force to be reckoned with in the world of literature and digital journalism. His work is a true testament to the power of creativity and the impact it can have on the world around us.

9 781917 267267